Advance Praise for a Twist of Lemon

Never underestimate the power of brevity. These stories are humorous, thought-provoking, and all-too-human. They are a delight to read!

~ Peter Goldsmith, Writer & TV Producer

Arlene Duane Hemingway's masterful creations, within the challenging format of microfiction, leave nothing out. They manage suspense, humor, deception, irony, and even tenderness, with intriguing characters and satisfying endings, in only 100 words! The stories in A Twist of Lemon address stirring themes including betrayal, entitlement, poetic justice, and love; the regrettable life choices and the emotions they elicit range from amusing to unsettling to cathartic and reaffirming. This is a superb collection for readers of diverse literary tastes.

~ Margaret Dinzler Shaw, Ph. D.,
Publisher, Writer and Editor,
Professor Emerita, Nassau Community College

I love your wicked wit! Arlene Duane Hemingway proves herself to be a gifted storyteller on many levels. Not only does she examine relationships in abundant variety, but she consistently manages this feat in exactly one hundred words. There are no extraneous adjectives to mar the frequently clever and startling outcomes. This collection of drabbles—as these short-short stories are called—is a must-read!

~ Marilyn McComas, author of the poetry collection *Palace of Imaginings*

A Twist of Lemon is refreshing and laser-like in its exploration of human character and personality. Arlene Duane Hemingway's artful words evoke strong emotions and colorful visual images. This provocative peek into the human condition made me, as it would any reader, reflect on life and wonder about relationships and paths chosen. Bravo! I'm looking forward to the next book!

~ Ann D'Angelo, Board Certified Coach, Owner of Transitions by Design

For those of you who might not be familiar with the "drabble," it is a unique and challenging literary form—a story not of 95 words, or 105 words, but of exactly 100 words. And Arlene Duane Hemingway has mastered the genre. Her drabbles give us a peek inside a variety of relationships and almost always end with startling ironies and clever turns that remind us that things are seldom as they seem. Herein lays Hemingway's wonderful talent. Much the way a lemon adds a twist of delight to a dry gin martini, readers who enjoy such artistic surprises will find a treasure in A Twist of Lemon.

~ Rand Bishop is a poet, writer and Fulbright Professor at the Universite Nationale du Gabon

A TWIST
OF LEMON

100 Curious Stories in
Exactly 100 Words

ARLENE DUANE HEMINGWAY

the three
tomatoes

The Three Tomatoes Book Publishing

First Printing: April 2020 Printed in the United States of America

ISBN-978-0-578-67007-2
Library of Congress Control Number: 2020905604

For permission requests, please address The Three Tomatoes Publishing, 6 Soundview Rd., Glen Cove, New York, 11542.

For my beloved grandfather
Thank you for your help.

"Reading is the sole means by which we slip,
involuntarily, often helplessly,
into another's skin, another's voice, another's soul."

– Joyce Carol Oates

INTRODUCTION

These microfiction stories are complete in one hundred words, from beginning to end. I'm passionate about writing them. A theme usually presents itself first, often followed by pre-named characters. At times, as a story evolves, characters alter their personalities, temperaments, and/or rename themselves. Surprisingly, stories I've considered completed have urged me to rewrite them.

An art form, called drabble, was developed in Great Britain in the 1980s. It was inspired by a word game suggested in Monty Python's *Big Red Book*. Players were to write a novel on a given theme. The winner was the first to finish. In the same decade, the Birmingham University of Science Fiction and others created the current 100-word version.

As an actual game, Drabble began to catch on. Writers including Isaac Asimov, Arthur Clarke, Terry Pratchett, and Neil Gaiman have tried their hand at them.

Because of their brevity, some people unfamiliar with the form assume drabbles are easy to write. This is frequently discovered not to be the case, after attempting to create one.

How to engage with this book? You can read one of these stories before bed, while drinking your coffee, or, to ease moments spent waiting for someone or something. Or, you can take one to your favorite discussion group! Covering a range of topics and emotions, they provide plenty of food for thought with enough love, hatred, malice, surprise, humor, deception, treachery, or mystery, for all.

Most of all enjoy them!

CONTENTS

At Summer's End

Laura remained in a fog. "I'm sorry," is all she remembered as George skulked away. No engagement. No bridal shopping. Unexpectedly, parental power had trumped love.

Two weeks later, ocean air enveloped her. George would've liked this, she reflected, viewing herself in a revealing string bikini. Quick pink toes stepping on hot sand, splashed at water's edge, moving deliberately beyond safety.

"Are you all right?" her rescuer asked after coaxing spurts of water from straining lungs. She nodded, shading sensitive eyes opened to fresh, harsh reality. Ocean sprays had replaced tear stains. Laura's ring finger bore summer's last tan line.

Conversation

A brakeless trailer had pushed Tom's motorcycle over the highway railing, killing him instantly. Every July 10th, for the following three years, his parents paid tribute on the front porch swing at 2:00 p.m. where and when they first heard the news.

Sally broke the silence. "He'd be twenty-five today."

"I know," Joseph replied, dabbing tears and gently holding her.

Overhead, the bright blue turned suddenly dark. By 2:45 p.m. the sun regained dominance of the "dirty sky," Tom's description of overcast conditions named at age three, accompanied by a fleecy procession.

"Tom's here?"

"Yes, but only for a moment."

The Decision

Extended crystal goblets, like tinkling bells, toasted the New Year. Allie examined each familiar face seen at holiday and *just because* parties, for more than a decade. *It's my pleasure* Bob became the official host for bowling team gatherings; he had a large house for entertaining and an Olympic-size pool.

Bill, Bob's whining twenty-eight-year-old perpetual-student son, was unsurprisingly disrespectful of women.

His off-color jokes became increasingly intolerable. Allie prayed she'd have a legitimate reason for not accepting any invitation until she could find the required team replacement.

After the twelfth stroke, only Allie knew her "Happy New Year" meant, "Farewell."

The Last Laugh

Arnold died suddenly. Entering the chapel, mourners were perplexed to find a room overflowing with flowers but no immediate family or casket containing the dearly departed.

The buzz of curiosity decreased when the funeral director began to make an announcement. "We're sorry about the delay. After the requested stop at Saint Mary's Nursing Home, where the uncle of the deceased paid his last respects, a massive traffic tie-up prevented the procession from arriving sooner. They're about five minutes away."

A voice from the back row was heard to observe, "Arnold had a wicked sense of humor and was always late."

A Good Investment

Mariela called the *Chronicle* to enquire about her missing newspapers. She was assured they'd been delivered, both days.

Positioning herself in the window the following morning paid off. A man she'd never seen before sprinted toward her lawn, hesitating just long enough to nick her paper.

Because it had solved her critter invasion problem, a friend suggested Mariela purchase a motion-activated sprinkler. Its range of thirty feet at a 120-degree angle was just perfect for a watery payback prior to the completion of the thief's next run.

For under seventy dollars, Mariela effectively controlled the critters on her property too.

Under Construction

"You get what you always get if you do what you've always done," was Cheryl's philosophy. Quality work plus changes to her physical appearance led to promotion from a cubicle to an office. But her clumsiness remained.

Rushing to her first corporate meeting, the spilled latte on her blouse necessitated a visit to the powder room. Presentable once again, Cheryl continued wiggling down the long hallway, past cubicles, ignoring former colleagues with whom she no longer chose to associate. Unfortunately, none of them informed her of her tucked-up slip.

After her unforgettable entrance, Cheryl was thereafter nicknamed *Ms. Southern Exposure*.

The Grass Is Always Greener

From his bedroom window, Jason watched his neighbors unload groceries while he disappeared yesterday's remaining pizza slice. At thirty-nine he envied the Bookers' fifty-year marriage—a relationship spiced with occasional honeymoon getaways.

Jason assumed his neighbors were naturally lucky. They weren't. Their hardships included a fire-gutted first house, the almost divorce when Garth's job required constant travel, and Bettina's postpartum depression. The Bookers' steadfast resolve to make things work was also unknown.

"Dinner," Jason's mother called from the kitchen.

"Thanks." Jason lumbered downstairs.

"Movie later, honey?"

"Yes, Mom." He sighed despondently.

"Nothing else to do," he muttered under his breath.

Boomerang

The eldest of four, Vesta, helped raise three brothers. Now grown, she was expected to continue maternal caretaking by raising her parentless infant nephew. The octogenarian grandparents were feeble and couldn't assist.

Vesta needed help. Her brothers responded, "We're strapped, and are so busy. You'll be fine. You're in our prayers."

Her boss had two small boys. She married him. Her permanent job assignment seemed pre-ordained: raising three boys full-time.

Vesta's brothers, during a downward spiral, requested help. Her husband responded, "We can't at the moment and have no time to spare. This too shall pass. We'll light a candle."

A Life on the Edge: Alpha

Kendra's penchant for things different and daring, and her desire to dominate, sky-rocketed after they met. Hoping for the best, Jay conceded to Kendra's playful wheedling regarding wanting a single rose tattoo. What followed were multiple provocative tattoos and body piercings, which Jay was expected to accept unconditionally, although he considered them distasteful.

If he'd followed his gut, Jay would've run when Kendra pursued him. But thrilling unlimited freeing sexual experimentation trumped common sense. Kendra was statuesque and mesmerizing.

Head over heels in lust, Jay tied the knot he sought to untie in eighteen months.

Their marriage soured so quickly.

A Life on the Edge: Omega

Eighteen months later, Jay realized Kendra had no boundaries regarding anything.

That frightened him.

Relieved not to find her in the apartment when he went to pick up his remaining belongings, Jay appraised the gun collection that had grown during their marriage, which was the only issue he had tried to stand up to her about.

Kendra entered carrying a nailed crate bearing a skull-and-cross-bones warning label.

He would never have guessed the contents. Although curious, Jay grabbed his things and left hurriedly without looking back.

Later, an over-confident Kendra fed her blue-ringed octopus. It delivered a painless, deadly bite.

The House Wins

Dereck tripped over misaligned elevator and hall sills. The prognosis of possible permanent paralysis from his waist down, plus excellent lawyering, left Dereck retired and wealthy.

He explained his physical situation and prognosis to Patricia over coffee. She still invited him to move in.

Dereck wasn't home while Patricia prepared for his birthday party, and installation of surveillance cameras, prompted by the rash of neighborhood break-ins. While she was at work the next day, he dallied, learning only of the scrutiny after Patricia's return.

Evidence showing Dereck grasping the call girl dispelled Patricia's paralysis concerns, but she evicted him nonetheless.

Wearing Sunday Best on Tuesday

Jim, a railroad man, summoned the courage to visit his neighbor. Declining to sit when invited, he thrust a dog-eared envelope at her. "Been thinkin' a long time, Bertha. I'd like a favor."

"What kind you want for all this money?"

"Li'l home cookin'. That's all. Wife's gone. Got no family."

Bertha paused, then smiled. "My pleasure."

Jim refused to take the money back.

Whenever Jim got home, he headed straight for Bertha's kitchen. After a year, Bertha told Jim she enjoyed his company but would stop cooking unless he stopped paying her.

After the nuptials, Jim paid for everything.

Sharing the Pain

This is Trina Gonzales in Babylon at the intersection of Route 109 and Montauk Highway in Lindenhurst where, an hour ago, Kenneth Wentworth made an illegal left turn. His Maserati GranTurismo Sport collided with a plumbing truck. Wentworth was thrown through the windshield. He died at the scene.

Just before he died, Wentworth claimed faulty brakes, but the half-empty bottle of Mondavi near the driver's seat indicated another possibility.

Mel, Kenneth's mechanic, watched the news without any expression. Three years ago today, Kenneth, high on Mondavi, had T-boned Mel's wife's car. She died instantly.

Now, Mel considers the scales balanced.

The Lesson

New employee Randy was invited by Brett and Greg to go drinking on Friday after work. For months this was routine until he asked his co-workers to cover his tabs, once too often.

After being scarce at work and a no-show on Fridays, Randy surfaced, apologizing for stiffing his co-workers and assuring them he'd settle-up this coming Friday, "If you can stand the sight of me."

Friday arrived. Unsuspecting Randy settled in at the bar. His phone rang.

"Hello!"

"We're pulling in now. Be a pal. Order our usual?"

"No problem. Bye."

Three drinks arrived. The two men never did.

Slam Dunked

Forced to turn down a sports scholarship to college, Angie reluctantly settled for a job to help support her ailing mother.

Two over easy, one small stack.

While grateful for their tips, six-foot-four Angie rebuffed overtures from gawking men watching her russet ponytail swing seductively. Basketball was her only love.

In the diners' parking lot, a storm-loosened awning toppled Angie and her bicycle. Although she was only bruised, an article about her caught the attention of a basketball coach interested in starting a new professional team.

The new team reaped benefits from ongoing PR.

Angie's contract solved her financial problems.

Educated Fingers

Galloping through his own inheritance, Wesley fast-forwarded an old friendship with Candace, a sightless heiress, into a romance. He fervently recited Byron's "She Walks in Beauty." They wed.

Clad in silk at their first dinner party, his shirt matched her dress. Aware of his pending *hot business deal*, Candice felt Wesley leaving as his phone rang.

After twenty-minutes he returned with a confident, "I sealed the deal." But he stammered when unable to quickly justify his change into a cotton shirt, after Candice's congratulatory hug.

Wesley was careless. He'd broken the infidelity clause in the prenuptial agreement.

The marriage dissolved.

Topsy-Turvy I: Duplicity

Conchita's references as a graphic designer, from former male employers, glowed. She seduced her new boss and befriended Angelina, the company's top designer.

After finding Angelina slumped in the stairwell, Conchita reported her missing. During Angelina's six-month recovery from a traumatic brain injury, Conchita transferred Angelina's complete files to her own home computer.

Angelina's claim to the projects, now managed by Conchita, were dismissed by their boss. He deemed it a matter of, "she said, she said." Now, many co-workers questioned Angelina's so-called accident.

Conchita blamed Angelina for her flat tire epidemic. Authorities dismissed it. "She said, she said" resurfaced.

Topsy-Turvy II: Subterfuge

Angelina fell in the office stairwell. Six months later she recovered from her traumatic brain injury, but not from fellow graphic designer Conchita pirating her files. Their boss dismissed Angelina's ownership claim. A case of, "she said, she said," he said.

Unknowingly, Conchita, Angelina, and husband, Rondell, rode the same Atlantic City charter. Angelina cried herself to sleep but awoke with a payback plan.

Rondell's concern for Angelina obscured the fact she was setting Conchita up.

Approaching restrooms, Angelina asked for money. Wallet-less, Rondell about-faced to search.

Angelina slipped his wallet into Conchita's stall, then texted Rondell.

Conchita was apprehended.

Topsy-Turvy III: It Took A Thief

Casino authorities questioned Conchita, victim Rondell, and his vengeful wife, Angelina. Conchita claimed that she'd found the wallet on her bathroom stall floor, and had been planning to turn it in.

Co-workers previously reluctant to label Conchita a thief, when accused the first time, changed their minds after her arrest. Some of them even concluded Conchita had a hand in Angelina's accident.

After incessant delays and changing court dates, Rondell dropped the charges. The case was dismissed. Conchita, now a victim of, "she said, she said," was fired.

Angelina attended mass more regularly and increased the number of confessional visits.

Everything Man

Harry's name came up whenever someone needed odd jobs or general upkeep done. In his mid-sixties, he established an excellent reputation by being affordable, efficient, on-time, and neat.

Being clean-cut, muscular, in great shape and ruggedly handsome were attractive bonuses. These attributes endeared him to a predominantly female clientele—older women living alone. Most were particularly well groomed for their appointments.

Happily married, Harry never made advances on his clients. But, had the opportunity arisen, more than one of them would have jumped without hesitation—especially Doreen who had a penchant for slightly bowlegged men. He was her fantasy cowboy.

A Case for Staying in Shape

Brenda qualified for membership in the *never put off until tomorrow what you can do today* club.

Today Brenda jogged, gardened, shopped, and prepared dinner. Disrobing to her underwear in the basement, she sorted clothes into the appropriate baskets.

Seeing her son's baseball cap reminded her that his equipment was still outside. The backyard was secluded. Capped Brenda raced to second, grabbed the mitt, scooped up the ball, then sprinted to home plate near the stairwell.

She froze when startled by the unexpected appearance of the landscaper.

He muttered under his breath, "You can certainly play on my team anytime."

Out of the Mouths of Babes

Alonzo, self-employed, usually came home late. Christina attended to all things domestic and home-schooled their son. Raphael's reading and computer skills were impressive.

He opened and read the first of two e-mails, with no hesitation. "Grandma sends me lots of love."

With Raphael now secured in the computer chair, Christina went to make a quick check on dinner. Hearing, "This one's from A-bri-en-da," made her spin around. She returned just in time to hear, "She's preg-nant and wants Daddy to stop ig-nor-ing her."

Alonzo now needs twice the business. He finances a house, his apartment, alimony, and double child support.

Daddy's Here

Guests gasped. At his eighth birthday party, Gerald prevented his mother from wiping frosting off his face with an omnipresent saliva-dampened tissue.

Gerald wasn't immune to his mother's closeted sobs and *I miss you Dave.* He was just getting older and wishing his father, now deceased for six years, was around to divert his mother's increasing clinginess. He hoped his father would have been proud of his taking *no football for a month* like a "real" man.

At bedtime, a familiar feeling of tingling hairs on the back of his neck lulled Gerald into peaceful slumber.

Tomorrow he would apologize.

Differing Opinions

After his daily park run, Shibli found a note on his windshield:

> Although we bear no resemblance, I respect Reverend Dr. Martin Luther King, even when it's not his birthday, as it is today.
>
> I see you as a vibrant child of God. We are the same. Our hopes, dreams, and prayers come from the same source. Yahweh!
>
> May the Great Benevolent be with you all of your days.
>
> Love and light,
> *Christopher*

When Shibli returned to his car in a church parking lot, that afternoon, he had four flat tires and a license plate stickered with a Confederate flag.

Lady-in-waiting I: The Fall

Gilbert, high on meth, suffered a paralyzing fall into the cellar. Amelia became her husband's caretaker and withdrawal coach.

Refusal to be a permanent lady-in-waiting in a loveless marriage prompted her immediate search for new caretakers. She mentioned plans to hire suitable assistance. Gilbert's, "You're supposed to take care of me!" shocked and angered her.

With everything in place for the last time, one year later to the day, Amelia eased out of bed without disturbing him. As Amelia was whisked from the airport to liberation in a Florida condo, Gilbert's morning nurse handed him an envelope containing divorce papers.

Lady-in-waiting II: Rebirth

Amelia's unpleasant reveries of ex-husband Gilbert's refusal to attend social events, before and after his accident and paralysis, were interrupted by a stranger's, "Hey Good Looking." She started smiling and continued walking, grateful her divorce was final.

After her hot bath, towel-wrapped and facing the mirror admiring the positive results of working out and getting plenty of rest, Amelia promised herself a full-body massage, and manicure and pedicure.

Over coffee, after her ballroom dance class, Amelia accepted her handsome dance instructor's invitation to go on a cruise. She was overjoyed being called *My Lady* instead of being considered Gilbert's lady-in-waiting.

Three Down

On the bus transporting seniors to high school graduation, Gloria prayed her family would come to the ceremony. They didn't. Gloria, the only student to ride the homeward-bound bus for guestless graduates, made school district history.

The following year, as brother Jessie crossed that stage, their father, attempting to stand, dropped from a shot to the neck. Jessie, accepting his diploma, succumbed to a bullet in the temple. Gloria's mother expired at the apron stage, shot between the eyes, clutching her camera.

College hadn't erased Gloria's years of emotional and sexual abuse. Her pistol, steadied by an avenging hand, tried.

In Plain Sight

Thief one, the bank guard, assured surveillance cameras were non-functioning. A lookout, parked directly in front of the bank with the engine running, discounted an unkempt man seated on a bench facing both bank and car. He wore dark glasses and held a short, white cane. Thief three, already inside, was signaled.

Seemingly forced at gunpoint, the guard helped empty the bank's coffers, separated customers from valuables, and helped pack the car before returning inside.

Realizing something was terribly wrong, the observer, only partially visually impaired, used his iPhone with voice-over and Siri to call 9-1-1.

Surprisingly swift apprehension followed.

His Heart Just Went

Sarah and Samuel, faithful to each other for sixty-five years, made people smile. Their hand-holding and fashionable attire caught everyone's immediate attention. Sarah made sure her husband wasn't *one of those saggy old men* who wore stained, ill-fitting clothes past their prime.

This morning, Samuel, who had never minded shaving, showering, or dressing *to look good for my queen*, needed help doing everything. He who had always stood straight, now stooped noticeably. In a few days, age had sneaked a massive withdrawal from his life account.

At Sarah's coffin, Samuel tearfully whispered a promise: "I'll meet you soon, my love."

Unexpected Plans

After graduating from different colleges, Scott and Jennifer, best friends since age three, went on a planned Caribbean get-away, with their parents.

All quickly donned bathing suits. The parents decided to go fishing. The graduates' opting out seemed reasonable. Comfortable with Jennifer's, "...just wanna lay back, relax, and enjoy it all," the graduates were left behind.

While fishing, the celebratory mood turned into silence. Jennifer's father had snagged Scott's red Speedo.

Discovering their impending parenthood, Scott and Jennifer sought jobs and house hunted.

'*Till death do us part*, a consequence of casual desire, assured no get-away for years to come.

Asked and Answered

Antonio died after a sumptuous Father's Day meal. With professional help, wife Sophia's emotional balance improved within six months. But Louisa, their belligerent twenty-five-year-old, live-at-home daughter, refused treatment.

One year later, mother and daughter visited the grave.

"I'm worried. Louisa has changed. She's so disrespectful and stays out most every night. You wouldn't have tolerated that. Louisa lost her job because of lateness. She's been jobless for almost a year."

I'm turning *your girl* over to you. Help me?"

When they returned home, they found Antonio's picture fallen from the wall. Louisa's old demeanor returned.

She soon got a job.

Arachnology I

Brilliant Monalisa, conceived on a couch beneath a print of the painting, admired black widows. Shiny black hair, bright red lips and nails, an hourglass figure, and silky black outfits earned her the nickname *Spider Woman*.

She only friended males; hopefuls stepped-up grooming and grades. Without thinking, those whose invitations she accepted willingly spilled intimate tidbits. Encounters ended with her gentle bite on their neck. Dreams of encores were dashed when unceremoniously unfriended. Word, and the line, got around. None thought of the improbability of black widows as friends with benefits or in committed relationships.

Today Monalisa's a premier dominatrix.

Slim Pickings

Slim caught weekend round-trip flights between his Pennsylvania home and New Jersey, where cousin Sandra provided room and board during Slim's airplane mechanic classes.

His breakfasts of six eggs and twelve strips of bacon tripled Sandra's food bill. So did bag lunches of prime leftovers or food clearly marked for Sandra's son. Slim ate whenever food was offered, even if he wasn't hungry.

Refusing to increase his contribution to food money, Slim announced he'd leave when exams were over *in just six weeks*. Sandra evicted him five weeks prematurely.

Angered by Sandra, Slim named his second impending ulcer after her.

Double Domination

Brady reluctantly confessed to a crime his three-strikes-you're-out brother committed.

After the strip search and shower, news of Brady's attributes rocketed around the prison. A war to *own* him started his unspeakable physical and psychological torment.

The victor in the battle, Brady's acclaimed *master,* arranged for his slave's infirmary stay. A tattoo artist inmate was present. Payoffs secured quarantined isolation, a diagnosis of pneumonia, and time for healing.

The sensationally executed tattoo, extending from Brady's shoulders to his buttocks, displayed a curvaceous, naked, long-haired woman. Each buttock had a carefully-centered nipple.

Shortly thereafter, Brady was moved to a padded cell.

When Mama's Not Happy

Yvonne, Pascal's new wife, displaced Champagne, his spoiled Chihuahua. The former first lady upped her barking. She scratched at the couple's closed bedroom door and was nightly banished to the sun porch.

Champagne clawed the bedroom drapes, urinated on the Persian rug, and chewed Yvonne's mother's antique settee. Now constantly growled at, Yvonne suggested hiring a pet behaviorist. Pascal ignored her. "My girls will eventually get along."

After learning her crystal wedding gift had been knocked off the coffee table, and shattered, Pascal's mother browbeat him into finding Champagne a new home.

Yvonne consoled her husband, through tears of joy.

Say Cheese

Although Mrs. *My-choices-are-simply-better-darling* Douglas controlled her daughter's life, Beth had found the man of her dreams without Mother.

Beth loved the venue, cake, and flowers. But weeks of gown shopping left her in tears because each of her choices was shot down.

In an intervention, Beth's friends convinced her to pretend to accept one of her mother's choices but actually purchase her dream dress.

Mrs. Douglas was visibly shaken upon seeing Beth at the church, and accepted two aspirin-look-alikes offered by a bridesmaid. Yawning commenced after the recessional.

Mrs. Douglas fell asleep during the reception.

Beth's day was picture perfect!

Advice Well Taken

After church, the Sunday prior to Thanksgiving, Jeremy disappeared from his mother's side.

Striding toward his aunt, he delivered an invitation, "*Please* come for Thanksgiving *this* year!"

Jeremy's mother unabashedly fabricated excuses for her sister. Today that was impossible.

"Yes, Hattie. You're Jeremy's *favorite* aunt."

Later, Jeremy learned Hattie was the by-product of his grandfather's affair, brought into the family after her natural mother died.

"Darling, some family members are best held at arm's length."

Upon securing his driver's license, Jeremy suddenly moved out of state. His mother set a place for him at the next Thanksgiving table, in hope.

Woman Scorned

Fernando agreed to be Lena's companion Friday through Sunday evenings.

On Friday afternoon he called in sick. She told him to rest and said she'd call him Saturday.

After working late Friday, Lena stops for take-out. Across the lot, she sees a young woman parking her car. Fernando instantly sprints from the passenger's side to open her door; they enter the restaurant holding hands.

After dinner, the woman, upset by finding her car keyed, ends their date early and drives Fernando home.

On Saturday, he tells Lena, "Still sick."

Lena provides plenty of time for recuperation: She lays him off.

"Thanks for Riding with Us"

August 8th

Mr. Frankie Frustrated
7 Railroad Avenue
Farmingdale, New York 11735

Re: MetroCard Serial Number: #3147953291

Dear Mr. Frustrated:

I'm responding to your request for a $2.50 refund, the cost of your additional MetroCard purchase, due to your malfunctioning $8.00 card.

My investigation found your original MetroCard malfunctioned, but wasn't permanently damaged. Enclosed is a new one in the amount of $0.25 (minus fees).

Your satisfaction is important to us. For further assistance, please contact us Monday to Friday, 9 a.m. to 5 p.m.

Sincerely yours,

Forever Unpersuadable

Forever Unpersuadable
Director, MetroCard Customer Service
Customer Services Division
Enc. #5911746038

Burdened

One phone call ended Lee's killing spree of young women. He was arrested and swiftly tried for capital murder. An insanity defense failed to win him a hoped-for life sentence.

The curtain at the state penitentiary opened to expose Lee strapped to a gurney.

All witnesses were journalists or victims' family members, except for Lee's lawyer and mother.

Tears bathed her chin. Her shoulders heaved. The handkerchief pressed to quivering lips, stifled truth verging on escape.

Although he couldn't see, Lee faced the viewing window and mouthed, "I love you, Mom."

The "anonymous" tipster took her secret to the grave.

Personals

"Did you know all septuagenarians don't just *stroll* in the park? I prefer sightseeing abroad, ballet, opera, love-making, reading aloud together, and back rubs. I'm statuesque, attractive, with a high energy level. Younger men apply. Must be levelheaded and physically flexible. Comfortable in various settings; social graces a must."

~Mrs. Robinson, Box 123.

"A semi-retired businessman who loves traveling, I prefer meeting a zesty older woman who is empowered, intelligent, attractive, experienced. At six feet seven, my clothes are Italian tailored. Have *all* my *own* hair. Let's talk."

~Fascinated Fifty-five, Box 218.

After one look, they become inseparable for years.

Baggage Squared I: His Mother's Son

Zachary willingly accepted full-time custody of the baby he didn't know wasn't his before Jamie-Lee refused to marry him. With papers signed, she suddenly disappeared. Walt was now legally Zachary's son.

Eighteen years later, Walt announced he was leaving to shack-up with a waitress, ten years his senior.

Tired of struggling while raising him alone, Zachary acquiesced to Walt's desire for freedom and independence. After sorrowfully releasing his son, he went into counseling himself.

Looking forward to erasing bitter memories and selling his current abode quickly, Zachary kissed the St. Joseph's statue, burying it upside down in the front yard.

Baggage Squared II: The Final Chapter

Standing in the doorway, Zachary's jaw dropped when his son appeared with assorted suitcases, boxes, bags, and an older woman, all begging entry.

"We have no place else to go, Dad." Walt didn't introduce the waitress with whom he had run off at age eighteen.

Zachary sighed. "It's been awhile."

"I've changed, Dad, I really have."

Zachary spoke with his eyes lowered. "The house just sold, son."

"Where are you......"

Walt never finished. He remained unnerved as Zachary, through silent tears, hugged him and the apparent mother-to-be.

The door locked. Refusing to look back, Zachary walked toward the waiting cab.

Green-eyed Monster

Gunther rebuffed Olga in junior high, favoring her younger sister Ingrid. Olga hated her for this until Ingrid left at twenty-one.

Sitting next to Olga, at Ingrid's party, Dad whispered to Olga, "Which is your gift?"

Upon hearing a spiteful, "*Just the pleasure of my company*," he spirited Olga out of the house, commanding she return with a gift or begin shouldering her own college expenses.

The envelope Olga slipped among gift boxes contained a card and three scratch-off lottery tickets. One thousand dollars a week for life was a winner.

Ingrid moved, paid her college tuition, and married Gunther.

It's Never Too Late

Marshall's heart pounded in anticipation of Ella's reaction to the surprise of red roses he sent, rather than his traditional spring bouquet. The phone rang. His "beautiful roses for a beautiful lady" sounded steady. Marshall's internal butterfly convention didn't betray him.

Octogenarian Marshall checked his Windsor knot before going to pick up his *gal* for their special dinner date.

Many patrons saw Marshall kneel. Holding his chair for stability, he retrieved a ring box from his pocket. Spontaneous applause erupted when Ella accepted his proposal.

Ella's bouquet of white roses complemented her lavender wedding dress. She looked stunning at eighty-two!

Problem Solved

Before last bell, Xavier lost his tooth. It went into a baggie provided by the school nurse. Thoughts of the Tooth Fairy and show and tell excited him.

Xavier held his breath while kissing Grandpa goodnight. Grandpa's soaking dentures on the bathroom sink sparked an idea. The dentures, now carefully drained and dried, were put under Xavier's pillow, with his own tooth.

Dear Tooth Fairy, please make Grandpa's garbage breath disappear. Amen.

After the note, Grandpa discovered white vinegar followed by peroxide to be a very effective cleanser.

At school, Xavier had five dollars to show and much to tell.

For Life

Now recovered, Paul recalled Judy's chicken soup, the gently tucked napkin, and cooling of each spoonful through beautiful pouted lips.

After locating her favorite recipe, Paul shopped while Judy slept.

Her tray contained lovingly prepared soup, fragrant sprigs of lavender, and a ready-to-be-tucked napkin.

Looking into the mirror, Paul spritzed aftershave and smiled at purposefully arranged strands of hair over one eye, an enticement for Judy to stroke with graceful fingers, nails artistically tipped in signature purple.

The couple cherished each other, considering every day so special it was never taken for granted.

Lovingly, they continued walking into forever together.

Like Father Like Son

Because Marcus Reinhardt was a political rising star, his family attended the event expecting to be scrutinized.

Instructed to be on his best behavior, five-year-old Elvis, Marcus' son, ran up to the talkative district leader's wife. He politely introduced himself as "the chip," then stuck out his hand.

"Nice to meet you, Mrs. Blah-mouth." He had heard his father, "the old block," use that term to describe her dozens of times.

Red-faced and apologetic, Marcus vowed to chastise his son and to "get to the bottom of this."

The Reinhardt's exited quickly.

Marcus' political aspirations had been "all shook up"!

Felis Domesticus Wisdom

They gathered where there was neither heat, tin, or a roof. The presiding Bobtail, one of the oldest among them, was scarred from experience. The youngest squeezed in front.

"Listen well:

1. Select laps of your choice.

2. Neither accept or acknowledge, "*No!*"

3. Get what you want by any means, then swagger away when you've had your fill.

4. Bristle, but never ever show fear.

5. Practice appearing and disappearing until *purrfected*."

At the next meeting, some now present would be gone, including the current sage.

Her replacement, a beautiful Bombay with piercing amber eyes, would be equally engaging.

Doctor, Doctor I: The Natural

Before the door opened completely, three-year-old Donna grabbed the bag her father, Damian DeVoe, internist, waved. She kissed him.

"Thanks, Daddy."

She put on the toy stethoscope then picked up the pen flashlight. Sitting down, Damian smiled. Donna's little fingers opened each of her father's eyes while carefully directing light into them. She then examined his nose, ears, and throat.

After resting her head on her father's chest for a while, she listened to his heart through her stethoscope. With the stethoscope now back in the bag, Damian asked, "What say you, Doctor?"

He chuckled at her, "You'll live," response.

Doctor, Doctor II: Dreams Realized

Dr. Damian DeVoe was ecstatic. His daughter would not be moving away after graduation from college.

Donna delivered the valedictorian address at her commencement exercises. Standing upright during the applause, Damian didn't hide his tears.

He remembered the examination she had given him with her toy stethoscope and pen flashlight, her head resting on his chest, and her pronouncement of, "You'll live."

Damian gave Donna three gifts. The first, a gold stethoscope-shaped pin. The second, boxed business cards. And the third, a shingle inscribed:
Dr. Donna DeVoe, Cardiologist.

This would hang next to her father's shingle:
Dr. Damian DeVoe, Internist.

Co-payment Magic

Shedding twenty pounds eliminated Sheila's desire to wear long tops as cover-ups. Joyously, she invested in new lingerie that would leave no visible panty-line.

But after noticing some mild groin discomfort, Sheila consulted her physician.

"How often do you experience this discomfort?"

"Sometimes once or twice a week. Sometimes more, sometimes less."

"Does it occur at a particular time of day; have you changed your diet or started a new exercise routine?"

"No, doctor."

After a brief examination, Sheila's physician left the room to regain her composure. Upon returning, she instructed Sheila on the proper way to wear a thong!

Too Little Too Late

Both Philippos and Denise considered marriage the ultimate goal. But after two years of declaring each other the *only one*, Philippos stopped short of fully committing.

His "give us more time" was unacceptable. Denise refused, and left. Realizing his mistake, he tried unsuccessfully to locate her.

Three years passed. Visiting out-of-state relatives, Philippos accompanied them to church. The new minister introduced his wife, stating, "This new assignment and meeting my wife were ordained by God."

A smiling Denise stood facing the congregation. She didn't notice Philippos.

More time hasn't decreased Philippos's remorse. He often remembers *the only one* for him.

Herstory in the Making

Claudette adjusted her wedding gown while rehearsing a speech Party Headquarters had requested of her, after returning from the honeymoon.

Overjoyed her "plain Jane" was getting married, the mother-of-the-bride led the shower ribbing about the wedding night and having babies. For her, a woman's place is in the home, and the words "wife and mother" are synonymous.

By contrast, Claudette was all about making political headway.

Twenty-five years later, defined by higher goals for womankind, Claudette campaigned for high government office. She annihilated her competition.

Claudette nodded toward her husband, proudly awaiting the official introduction as America's first Madam President.

Working the Fetish

When a girl at the beach playfully threw a flip-flop at the boy chasing her, she missed. It landed, instead, on the crotch of thirteen-year old T-Bone who was lying on his back, basking in the sun.

But by quickly turning onto his stomach, he hid his involuntary physical reaction. Embarrassed, he accepted her apology, while hiding his face.

For the rest of the summer, T-Bone lived at the beach, blissfully combining print and visual research. The incident had aroused an inexplicable interest in women's feet and footwear.

After acing his college and graduate studies, T-Bone became a dedicated podiatrist!

Over the Edge

Her son's engagement to Kiko enraged Zipporah. His father's affair with, and subsequent marriage to, a Japanese woman was still fresh.

Now composed, Zipporah offered the couple help with wedding plans. After politely refusing, they eventually accepted her offer to host the wedding dinner, but only if Zipporah gave the assurance that an invitation to her ex *and* his wife would be sent.

While conversation about Kiko was minimalized, Zipporah gushed about *her* dress for the wedding. Her ex-husband's wife arrived at the dinner wearing its double.

Zipporah revisited her closet for another outfit.

Therapy failed to lift her depression.

The Other Woman

Monday through Friday, passengers of the second car on the 6:37 a.m. commuter train anticipated the entrance of a voluptuous redhead favoring tight turtlenecks and pencil skirts. With coat removed and hair fluffed, she looked for her regular seatmate, a clean-cut man in business attire wearing a Rolex.

On this day, she sat next to him, promptly starting a lively conversation. Once outside the station, they flagged a cab, jumped in and embraced.

Two days later, Detective Bowen, hired by the man's suspicious wife, documented the affair. She filed for divorce. So did Detective Bowen. His wife was the redhead.

Happy, Happy

With the mortgage paid, Darwin pestered Frieda about purchasing a boat. She considered this unrealistic. Her priority was refurbishing their outdated surroundings.

A six-month plan was secretly forged. Frieda completed the remodel aided by do-it-yourself shows, online discounts, thrift shops, talented friends, and a storage pod, all while Darwin was out of town.

Upon his return home from an annual fishing contest, Darwin was impressed by the innovative changes and awed by a newly created man cave.

Darwin's dream was also realized. The couple's increased social interaction led to his purchase of a budget-friendly, pre-owned vessel from a new friend.

Interpretation Mishap

Adele and Stanley, new teachers in the same school, never dated. But she felt comfortable asking her friend to accompany her to the annual faculty picnic since neither had a date.

Stanley opened her car door after placing the picnic basket in the trunk.

At day's end, as Stanley placed the picnic basket on her countertop, Adele thanked him for being a perfect gentleman.

Stanley entered the living room.

Throughout the day, Adele's sandals made her grimace. She excused herself to *get more comfortable*, returning to find gentleman Stanley on the couch stripped to his briefs.

She'd changed her shoes.

Hiding Place

Unlike the virile father whose name he bore, pale and sickly Francois was spoon-fed helpings of, "You're pathetic," from birth.

He left home bearing permanent stripes of worthlessness, incapable of believing his scientific brilliance. But astrophysics research companies recognizing it lavishly courted him.

Navigating his office with Zen-like precision, Francois could pluck needed references off shelves by touch, not sight.

He avoided family and/or holiday celebrations. He doggedly resisted attempts by well-intentioned souls to break him out of his concrete shell. Considering social interaction fraught with painful variables, Francois' structured world remained his salvation.

His birthright of denigration was impenetrable.

Insult Added to Injury

Bernard, age thirty-five, had no contact with his father ever since being called a *freeloader*, and told, "Move out and find a job."

After his father became bedridden, Bernard ignored multiple requests to contact him.

For six years, newly retired, deferring personal dreams, Anne became her father's devoted caretaker.

Bernard didn't attend the funeral. Shortly thereafter, Bernard learned he had been his father's only beneficiary.

Bernard and his sister had never gotten along. After deciding to move into *his* mortgage-free house, Anne, now sixty-seven, was told, "You may stay as long as you like, until you find your own place."

Reveille

Trish became sleep-deprived herself from having to nudge her "comatose" sleep-apneic husband, Prince, so many times, each night. A pulmonologist's evaluation indicated he'd done this a whopping six-hundred times during his six-hour sleep apnea test.

Besides cleaning his C-Pap machine, which Trish refused to touch, Prince's daily routine consisted of reading the paper, watching television, and waiting for meals to be served.

One morning, when not smelling the usual comforting aroma of coffee upon awakening, Prince nudged Trish lying next to him. After finding her cold to the touch, he panicked. Overworked and underappreciated, she'd peacefully expired during the night.

No Forwarding Address

Ruth allowed her "temporarily" jobless brother to share her apartment. When asked about his progress, Lucky was "still hanging in there," or "this close." After a year of returning home each evening, still unemployed, Ruth wised-up.

She accepted an overseas promotion, which included a salary increase, a house, and payment of all moving expenses. On escape day, Ruth told Lucky not to come home before dinner so the landlord could finish painting the rental. Unsuspicious, he left after a substantial breakfast.

Lucky returned to an empty apartment except for the sofa bed with a note attached.

RENT DUE, TWO WEEKS.

Goo-goo-da-da

Since becoming a grandma, Virginia quickly realized she was expected to baby-sit weekend evenings for her son and daughter-in-law, usually without courtesy of advance notice. Tired of being taken advantage of, Virginia explained to her son that occasional babysitting was fine but a reliable long-term plan was needed.

Her admonishments fell on deaf ears.

The following Saturday evening, Virginia answered the door wearing a red satin robe and high heels. Her hair was disheveled, and, except for smeared lipstick, her make-up perfect.

Before closing the door, after taking a sip of wine, Virginia purred to the startled couple, "Not tonight."

Cherished

On her 100th birthday, Agnes was escorted to the head of a festive dining room table. She remembered all of the attendees' names. Time mercifully spared her mental acuity, claiming instead the perfect spine, now bent into the shape of the letter *C*.

Pearl, Agnes' latest great-great-grandchild, lay quietly in her lap, looking up at her. Agnes kissed her, and then whispered something no one else would ever hear but would always wonder about.

Agnes considered this day to be the best one of her life. She died peacefully in her sleep at 102.

Pearl never forgot the secret message.

Sexy

"This is Mrs. Tarnover. We met in Yoga class."

Nodding politely, Richie kissed the extended hand. "The pleasure's all mine."

"Would you believe she just celebrated her seventy-fifth birthday? I finally know somebody who's older than I am."

Everyone chuckled.

Surely there was some mistake Richie thought, stepping back for a closer look at his grandmother's hot new friend. Mrs. Tarnover smiled as she gently withdrew her hand.

"What are you ladies up to?"

"I convinced Beverly to take out a personal ad before she gets cold feet. She wants my help in composing it."

Richie subscribed to the newspaper.

Happily Married

"Rochelle's much broader now since lunching with the gals."

"I know what you mean. Esther had a twenty-one-inch waist. Now you can just about double that."

"Sadie's bunions prevent her from wearing those sexy high heels anymore."

Not desiring to participate in this too-much-to-drink Man Circle ritual, Milton excused himself. After such events, Milton was grateful for wife Myrna and happy he'd be leaving the party with her. He couldn't imagine her not beside him when he awakened each morning. Milton now valued having been tutored by sisters and thankful for not letting Myrna go when some inquired, "Why her?"

Her Piano Man

On her first visit to the club, Verna caught the pianist's fancy. She believed their ensuing relationship was exclusive until Russell suddenly left for good.

Months later, a new club featured him on keyboard. Verna arrived during his introduction of his singer bride. Verna snapped. She began stalking Russell.

Russell's set-break cigarette ended with a fatal blow to the head. Verna transported his body to her work. After being treated to a four-hour roast at 1,700 degrees Fahrenheit, Russell's pulverized ashes were carefully sifted into the murder weapon, a heavy, piano-shaped urn.

Verna, a crematorium specialist, encapsulated Russell for eternity.

Blissful Ignorance

The assembly of new renters in Suite A, twenty shapely young women, registered as a belly dancing class. Danny, the janitor, nicknamed them "The Boa Club" because of the feathered accessories attached to their large canvas carryalls.

Danny, looking forward to ogling, was disappointed when denied entry during the classes because "some women might feel uncomfortable."

When doors locked, dancers reached for their bags. Contact aroused movement in each. Opened bags revealed slithering contents which—after careful extraction—were draped around their owner's bodies.

The music ended as the routine undulated to a serpentine climax that Danny couldn't have imagined.

Silent Departure

Blane returned from another expedition to supplement his low-wage job. Kennat shouted, "I won the Medical Lottery!"

Just then, a familiar face on television startled her; the newscaster spoke:

> *Dr. Woodrow Claxton, founder of the Medical Lottery Program, was discovered dead in his hotel room. Earlier, he'd delivered an address encouraging physicians to give to their communities. He'd scheduled another pro-bono heart surgery tomorrow.*

Blane tearfully placed his gun, some jewelry, and cash on the table.

Kennat, deprived of otherwise unaffordable surgery by a heist gone wrong, picked up the gun, killed him, and then turned the gun on herself.

Mid-life Crisis

Anderson walked on stage to generous applause and a few whoops. He adjusted the microphone and said, "How y'all?" to the audience.

"Guys, don't you wish you were as perfect as your wives? If my wife was sitting out there you'd see how lucky I am. But Liberty's home, resting. One of us has to earn a dependable living."

The year before, mired in middle-age and without prior discussion, he'd cavalierly quit a lucrative job to pursue comedy full-time. She had not supported his dream.

Year two rolled around. Separated and broke, not-so-funny Anderson moved back in with his parents.

A Fly in the Ointment

Buddy, a wannabe trendsetter at fifteen, dressed for school in super-low baggy jeans, and sneakers, which he left untied.

"Pull your pants up. Tie those laces."

Buddy responded, "Yeah, yeah," and slammed the door.

While selecting a cafeteria table, Buddy tripped on a shoelace. He slipped on some spilled soda and lay sprawled on his scattered lunch consisting of chicken nuggets, over-saturated coleslaw, and greasy fries. When Buddy stood, his jeans descended to his ankles. The zipper had broken.

When hearing about the incident, Buddy's mother showed loving concern. But he wondered about the uproarious laughter from the laundry room.

Endangered Species

Jackson, age seventeen, is laid out in his only suit and tie.

In sweltering summer heat, this humble sanctuary is packed. Open windows and ceiling fans are weak substitutes for the nonfunctioning air-conditioning system. With worn maroon carpeting and water-stained walls a backdrop, city officials stand out like undissolved marshmallows in cocoa.

The eulogy, based on a scathing newspaper article—ANOTHER CHILD SURRENDERED TO DEATH—details the circumstances underscoring the rising epidemic.

Jackson's mother faints. Lincoln, Jackson's nineteen-year-old cousin and closest friend, is pried away from the casket, after the viewing. The odds are Lincoln won't live to see twenty-one.

Varoom

Flirting with a female driver in a car alongside him, Winston plowed his Harley into the back of a truck. Time had caught up with him, altering his reality forever. Six months later he could walk again, but the use of his hands was limited and burn scars permanently disfigured his attractive appearance.

One of his close friends suggested that he consider getting into politics. Winston led the rounds of hysterical laughter. Finally, after regaining his composure, Winston feigned seriousness, posing a hypothetical winning tagline: "I'm not just another pretty face."

Laughter erupted again. But a seed had been planted.

Poor Baby

Charlie inherited his father's love of the vintage automobile that shared garage space with the family sedan. His father, when eight, started driving Baby on the farm. Informed of this at ten years old, Charlie pestered his father to teach him to drive at Grandpa's farm.

After coming across the hidden keys to Baby, ecstatic Charlie yielded to temptation. He called Red, his next-door partner in crime. "Come quick. No one will be home until late."

Baby was started, reversed, over-accelerated. Neither boy was hurt, but Baby and the garage door sustained massive damage.

Charlie's grounding began. His pestering ceased.

Side by Side

Before going to the facility, Claire dressed in her husband's favorite color, blue. On the nightstand lay a sealed envelope.

Today, after having no signs of conscious activity for two-and-a-half years, Wallace's mechanical ventilator would be unplugged. Legal authorization, and having neither children nor close relatives, eased the process.

Alone with him, after locking the door and dimming the lights, Claire took her hair down, and then swallowed the contents of two vials. After tenderly kissing Wallace, she replaced his wedding ring and lay down next to him, touching her ring to his, both etched by fifty years of constancy.

No Complaints

Honey didn't work. She had a personal trainer and went to the gym daily. She and her husband, Harvey, lived in a large old Victorian, which justified the plumber's truck, the gardener's truck, the electrician's van, the contractor's van, or the handyman's van, and their frequent appearances on Tuesdays or Wednesdays. The maids came on Mondays and Thursdays. Fridays were reserved for private maintenance including a massage, facial, and hair and nail appointments.

After work, Harvey hurried home to his alluringly attired, or unattired, Honey, who always made him feel so very special—after five, weekdays, and all weekend long.

Not Taking the Bait

Robin and Mercy's parents emphasized good grades, employment after college, and financial independence.

Robin married a man equally devoted to making their money outlive them. They started a family. After high school graduation, Mercy quit school to marry her child's father.

Her response to Robin's news of fourth-stage cancer was cavalier. "Sorry. But, I've got bad news too. Ryder's HIV devours our finances." Mom and Dad can't contribute forever. And, Ryder's pension dies with him. The house is our only asset. Help! Include me in your will."

Once recomposed, Robin responded. "Sorry. But if you outlive Ryder, sell your asset."

Zilch!

Victor texted his wife, who was delighted he'd be driving her new car home after his "dinner business meeting." Not minding he'd be first to put mileage on it, she praised his thoughtfulness.

At the restaurant, Victor's middle-aged mistress, Hillarie, crossed the parking lot. She, a first-year employee at his car dealership, convinced him to let her drive the car around the block after dinner. They hit a pole. Hillarie was no longer a secret. There were police probes, medical bills, and lawsuits; her work career was over.

There would be no fifth seven-year-itch for Victor, D.O.A. at age sixty-eight.

Jumping to Conclusions

The housekeeper took time off to heal from knee surgery.

Neal and wife, Ada, attended a benefit gala. After the party, he helped his inebriated wife get ready for bed. Ada had placed her antique diamond and sapphire drop earrings on the dresser, not back in her safe, as was usually the case. Neal didn't know the combination.

Winter, a temporary replacement, began work the day after the party. After Winter, cleaned the bedroom, Ada realized her earrings were missing.

Winter tearfully professed her innocence. Neal dismissed her anyway.

He smiled, having seized a golden opportunity to supplement his allowance.

No Stopping Him

On the hottest day in years, following a month-long drought, a long line of limousines carried the famous and infamous to the cathedral for the funeral of a larger-than-life financier. The exquisite floral tributes paled next to his gilded casket.

Later, at the interment, the winding mechanism lowering the coffin malfunctioned. Horrified attendees witnessed the casket's eerie non-stop plunge well beyond the anticipated pre-dug six-foot limit. The widow fainted. The priest couldn't look and crossed himself several times over.

The deceased, often laughingly, attributed his success to his bargain struck with the Devil. Today, those who recalled it didn't laugh.

Distracted

Clinton was a womanizer. Walking his dog in the park was enjoyable. It was exercise and a favorite pickup spot for meeting many available, attractive women.

Engaged in conversation with one such prospect, he was clueless about being entangled by his dog's leash as it investigated her dog.

Numbers were exchanged. As the woman walked away, Clinton's eyes followed her briefly before he attempted to move on. But because of his predicament, he was unable to do so and fell into the pile of his own dog's poop.

Unfortunately, many women noticed Clinton that day. He wished he was invisible.

Truth Will Out

High school sweethearts, Felicity and Salvatore, pledged to remain virginal until their wedding night. Now married and raising teenage boys, Salvatore received a letter from a man claiming Salvatore was his father. Salvatore had never revealed his continued molestation by a high school teacher.

Wanting to be a good husband and father, and fearful that the letter's author might try to find him, Salvatore read the letter to Felicity. Afterward, he expressed his shame and embarrassment.

Felicity knew Salvatore was blameless and insisted that he attend her next therapy session, when she revealed her molestation by the same female teacher.

Study War No More

Based on the animosity between their countries, two thirtyish singles rejected each other's profile on a dating site to which both subscribed. They were unaware of each other's proximity until they bumped elbows in their Baltimore apartment elevator.

Basher, an accountant born in Palestine, loved tennis, hiking and Chinese cookery. Shira, a veterinarian born in Israel, loved tennis, hiking, and eating but not cooking Chinese.

The jostling caused Shira to drop her takeout bags from Asia Wok. Basher apologized profusely while escorting her to her door.

The wedding took place on the anniversary of their collision, the following Valentine's Day.

Sins of the Mother

Lionel's father collapses while viewing him in the hospital nursery. His mother, resenting being stuck raising him without a husband, supplies basic care in a loveless setting. Books are the only friends Lionel makes.

At 10:00 p.m., a limousine transports Lionel to a government facility. His proofreading job, cloaked in secrecy, requires perfection. The solitude nurtures him. He's home by 7:00 a.m.

On his twenty-seventh birthday, Lionel finds an open note wishing him a nice life. His mother's door keys are taped to the bottom of it.

Newly alone, Lionel keeps the apartment. His new housemate is one-hundred-proof guaranteed solace.

No More Visits to the Farm

John's parents never knew Uncle Hank sexually
abused him during a late-summer farm visit.
His new obsessions regarding privacy and locking
and double-checking the bathroom door were
attributed to starting kindergarten.

In high school, John showed no interest in women;
he declared chastity and his intention to become
a priest.

Visitors assembled at Hank's deathbed made room for
Father John. Hank couldn't speak.

John offered Hank Holy Communion, which he
accepted. After John dampened a ricin-laden wafer and
placed it between Hank's parted lips, he whispered,
"God have mercy on our souls."

Father John left just before succumbing to nausea.

G.I. Joe

Peter lionized his father and never tired of listening to his war stories. Once gifted with his father's dog tags, he never removed them. Directly after high school graduation, Peter enlisted in the Army.

Realizing the tags would be taken at the induction site, he sadly removed them, and lovingly placed them in the glove box. His father discovered them six months after Peter's deployment but didn't tell his wife because she was experiencing sharp pains in her chest.

A few weeks later, two notification team officers, in Class A dress uniforms, emerged from a government vehicle with heart-wrenching news.

Behold the Changing Goose

After a few years of married life, Henry became His Majesty. He no longer kept in shape but insisted his wife, Nadine, remain size zero. Her birthday and their anniversary, no longer considered important, were conveniently forgotten.

Henry flaunted his dominance by becoming drunk, often touching Nadine shamelessly in front of friends.

Once again, Nadine received a familiar text: "I'll be working late."

Arriving at a restaurant with a female *client*, he became agitated after spying his wife dining with a striking, sober, six-packed escort.

Later that evening, feathers flew in the castle. His Majesty was demoted to Prince Henry.

Morning Rewards

The path narrowed as Daria felt the dawning sun on her left shoulder. With enough light to feel safe and enjoy the grassy dew, gleaming like diamonds beside gravel park pathways, she began her daily walk.

A tall young man ran in lockstep close behind an equally tall young woman. They didn't converse, but Daria sensed they were life partners. She wondered if *she* felt *his* support as Daria felt Vincent's, whenever they walked together. Heading for home, she looked forward to a leisurely bath followed by a delicious breakfast. Vincent, her spouse of thirty-years, always prepared both for her.

Farewell Forever

Things became unbearable when Malavita's mother confronted her husband about the abuse. Denying accusations, he called her a liar. The eleven-year-old was suddenly shipped to out-of-state relatives.

Malavita only returned to the house once, when attending her mother's funeral 20 years later. She blamed her father for her untimely death.

Now, at forty-three, memories of her painful past still haunted her.

Dry-eyed, Malavita waited until the last guest left the gravesite. She walked to the soon-to-be-filled void, paused, turned, and returned to her car. No rose was offered.

From a distance, she relished each shovel of dirt, especially the last.

You Can Count on a Pig

After their son died, Ox began binge-drinking and manhandling his wife. Tormented by, "You should have died instead," eye-blackening escalated. After prolonged patience and attempts at reasoning failed, Bonnie took control of the situation.

Before Ox vanished for good, he'd begun staying away from their hog farm for days at a time. Bonnie often reported him missing, so authorities never doubted her sincerity regarding finding him this time.

Searches proved unsuccessful.

Ox's shaved, indigestible hair was disposed of. His remains, carefully disseminated and micro-managed among the sties, supplemented the hogs' corn and soybean mixture.

Bonnie's fat porkers fetched top prices.

Ungratefuls I: They Blew It

Alfred and Bernice met in college. They majored in partying. Bernice became pregnant. After she quit school, her parents made an acceptable offer: get married, receive a three-week honeymoon, a condo, stipends including child care costs, and sweetheart job opportunities.

For six months, Alfred was a no-show for several interviews, late or inappropriate on others. The downwardly mobile couple were neither employed nor re-enrolled in school.

While living comfortably for another year, they turned deaf ears to all lectures pertaining to personal responsibility.

After Alfred and Bernice aged-out of family health insurance coverage, stipends stopped.

Their gravy train had derailed.

Ungratefuls II: Fed-Up

Alfred saw no need to contact his blue-collar mother, Isabelle, while living on his in-law's largess.

Now, since the stipends ended, he planned a surprise family visit. On the way, he spotted his mother's car entering a restaurant parking lot. After parking next to her, Alfred hurried to quickly grab his daughter.

Isabelle barely exited before Alfred thrust the child toward her. "Here's your granddaughter. Don't you want to hold her?" Isabelle didn't and stepped back as Bernice attempted a hug.

Anticipating a pitch for scot-free something, Isabelle wasn't about to become a sucker. She invited them for lunch instead.

Ungratefuls III: The Last Supper

When first greeting Isabelle, Alfred hadn't bothered to say hello. During dinner, however, he was at his most charming.

As Alfred gorged on expensive menu items, Isabelle asked about his future. He spun a tale of not having had enough time to turn his life around but implied things were improving as of late. This continued while Isabelle delivered her personal-responsibility lecture.

Predictably, Alfred kept rolling his eyes.

After signing the credit card slip, Isabelle stood, hugged the baby, and tenderly kissed each of them. She excused herself but never returned to the table.

The waiter handed Alfred a note.

Ungratefuls IV: Bye-bye

My Dear Son,

Your news of being on the verge of change and improving your life circumstances warms my heart. I'm rooting for you!

I'm going away very soon and won't be back.

I will always pray for you.

Love,
Mom

Surmising Isabelle was dying, Alfred hurried his family into the car and sped to his mother's address. A cleric was opening the door to the house Alfred thought would be his soon. But his assumption was incorrect. Isabelle donated her property to the church.

Confused, Alfred calls his mom, whose phone was disconnected. He was now on his own.

Ungratefuls V: New Woman

The interruption by Alfred and his family caused Isabelle to scrap her plan to make an important decision over a quiet dinner. Instead, she invited her son and his family to dine, during which something became painfully clear.

She knew any temporary financial life-line to Alfred would lead to expectations of its permanency, as any family member was an available pawn to satisfy his entitlement.

Isabelle left not telling Alfred she was the latest Australian lottery winner. As a British citizen, she was guaranteed public anonymity regarding her elevation from blue-collar status.

Her coffers overflowed. Alfred didn't get a dime.

Legacy I: If Not for Their Mother's Love

Three twenty-something sisters pulled up their Mississippi farm roots and exchanged life as Dad's indentured servants for freedom and a Bronx apartment. They all married and moved within two years, making it easy for their mother to alternate residences, since she also left their father.

Mom died contented, knowing her girls were thriving in *cage-free existences*, a reference to years of chickens they'd fed, coops they'd cleaned, and eggs they'd collected.

Each granddaughter, in turn, respected her mother's journey. All became confident, independent women and revered the grandmother they'd never met who had secretly saved money for their mothers' escape.

Legacy II: Powerless Potentate

After his wife left the Mississippi chicken farm to live with their daughters in the Bronx, Franklin raged at their impudence for leaving without his permission. He ruled the roost!

Franklin's granddaughters thrived on the love of a mother and father—something his daughters never had while growing up.

Family attempts to contact him ceased when he failed to respond to the funeral program they had sent of their mother's service. Unmoved, he intentionally missed an opportunity—his last—to make amends.

Declaring his family dead, Franklin never uttered their names aloud again.

But his memory stubbornly refused to fade.

Parlaying a Little Knowledge

Rhianna noticed the clean-cut and well-dressed man whenever he entered the elevator from the floor housing a prestigious law firm. Unaware that the attorney business card Warren gave her was bogus, she invited him for drinks.

Rhianna had an awakening after Warren's withdrawals for personal expenditures from their joint checking account increased in disproportion to his contributions. Fortunately, she jumped on emptying the account and had him investigated, barely prior to him saying, "I've been terminated."

Warren moved out and then immediately in with a still wealthy, for now, but very dependent woman who thought he was a physical therapist.

Order in the Court

Rage preceded Yang's lunge at Morty, his never-apprehended rapist, while both awaited trial—Yang for shoplifting, Morty for child molestation. Their first encounter happened when Yang was ten.

Yang's handcuffs didn't prevent him from inflicting serious injuries to Morty's head and testicles.

Yang was lucky. The shoplifting charges he'd pleaded innocent to were dismissed. So were the assault charges at his later trial, due to his impassioned defense, "For twelve years, I've been paying for the harm he inflicted on me."

Convicted of molestation charges, Morty experienced pain for life, which wasn't long after being labeled a pedophile in prison.

ACKNOWLEDGEMENTS

Sincere thanks to Judy Turek, co-leader of writing workshops at the Farmingdale Library in New York, for introducing me to this genre. Her encouragement, "Write on," is always with me.

Sincere thanks to Ray Russell, Mike Hopping, and the broader membership of the Writers' Group of Asheville, North Carolina, for helping me focus on essentials.

Sincere thanks to Lynn Komlenic, my skillful editor and literary ombudsman.

Sincere thanks for the smiles of anticipation from members of the Writer's Forum of the First Congregational UCC of Hendersonville, for people's recognition of me outside of a reading venue, to those who share feedback with me on experiences or incidents they've been reminded of through my stories, and for the creative projects these stories have inspired.

BIOGRAPHY

After graduating with a Master of Science Degree from Juilliard School of Music with a major in organ, Arlene Duane Hemingway became a private piano teacher, and a vocal music teacher in a Long Island public school system. She also served as an organist and choir director for religious services of various faiths. Arlene performed with the Mormon Tabernacle Choir at Radio City Music Hall, worked numerous other musical events in New York, and helped launch a composer's new work at the Lincoln Memorial in Washington, DC.

Following her professional retirement from music, Arlene concentrated on other healing arts. She is a certified hypnotherapist and Reiki Master and holds additional certifications in Regenesis (a method of reprogramming DNA), along with other techniques. During a visit to a writer's group in Farmingdale, NY, Arlene discovered the "drabble," a short work of fiction of precisely one-hundred words in length. She was hooked! A recent move to the Asheville, North Carolina area gave her more room to breathe, listen, and write.

When asked about a relationship to Earnest Hemingway, her reply is often, "I'm the other Hemingway—the one without the six-toed cats." Arlene has discovered that every person, place, or thing is rich with stories wanting to be told ... and she has just scratched the surface.

Arlene can be contacted through The Three Tomatoes at info@thethreetomatoes.com.

01.21.2021 1016